Testimony

Thank you for saving our family! J.H.

.....

"Lois was a great benefit to me and to my late husband, Bill. From the first time we met Lois, we knew we were in Good Hands. I consider her to be a friend as well. I would highly recommend Lois to anyone finding themselves in need of a true professional. M. K.

.....

As the Director of Geriatric Care Management, Lois Tager provides an invaluable service for her clients. During a very difficult time when a family members' health was declining, we were faced with arranging for long term care and medical assistance, having no idea where to start we contacted Lois. We consider ourselves extremely fortunate that Lois was available and felt immediate relief when Lois demonstrated her knowledge, experience and compassion while addressing our needs. Lois not only prepared and submitted all required forms for medical assistance but also assisted us in researching long-term care facilities.

On an as needed basis, we continue to call upon Lois for her assistance.

We want to thank her for the services she has provided for so many families including ours. Thank You!! N. H. & S. H.

.....

"Thank you so much Lois, for your help and support!! We couldn't have done it without you! You made our Mom so very happy! L. L.

What To Do
with Your Stuff

What To Do
with Your Stuff

A Guide to Decisions About Personal
Possessions and Life Choices

by

Lois G. Tager M. Ed., CSA

Publisher's Note

This publication is designed to provide generally helpful information on the subjects discussed, however it is not a substitute for the professional advice needed to suit your specific circumstances. It is sold with the understanding that the publisher and author are not engaged in rendering professional or legal advice or any other professional services.

References are provided for informational purposes only and do not constitute endorsement of any web sites or other sources. If advice is needed, a competent professional in your area should be engaged.

Lois G. Tager

5339 Prospect Road No. 211
San Jose, CA 95129   www.whattodowithyourstuff.com

Ordering Information

Quantity sales. Special discounts are available on quantity purchases by corporations, associations, and others. Please contact us by going to www.whattodowithyourstuff.com

Individual sales. What To Do With Your Stuff is available through most bookstores. The book can also be ordered directly throught the website www.whattodowithyourstuff.com

Orders for college textbook/course adoption use. Please contact us through the website www.whattodowithyourstuff.com

Printed in the United States of America

What To Do With Your Stuff was printed in the United States. When it is available, we choose paper that has been manufactured by environmentally responsible processes. These may include using trees grown in sustainable forests, incorporating recycled paper, minimizing chlorine in bleaching, or recycling the energy produced at the paper mill.

Tager, Lois G.
    What to do with your stuff : a guide to decisions about personal possessions and life
        choices / by Lois G.
    Tager, M. Ed., CSA.
    pages cm
    Includes bibliographical references and index.
    ISBN 978-0-9908421-0-1

    1. Older people--United States. 2. Personal belongings--United States--Decision making.   3. Moving, Household--United States. 4. Estate planning--United States--Popular works. 5. Personal property--United States--Popular works.   I. Title.

    HQ1064.U5T344 2014   646.7'9

                    QBI14-2145

Book Producer & Designer—Jimmie Young/Tolman Creek Media

Dedication

To my amazing, supportive and loving husband of forty years,
who never said "you can't" but always said "go for it"
and allowed me to believe I could accomplish anything.

And to our incredible children and grandchildren,
you light up my life.

Acknowledgments

Do you believe that some things are just meant to be? I do and it never ceases to amaze me when they actually happen. In 2009, while helping to take care of my 93 year-old mother-in-law, I decided to open my own practice as an advisor to seniors since I had been working with seniors for a very long time. While studying for my Certified Senior Advisor exam, I received a newsletter from the Law Offices of Roy W. Litherland, an Elder Care Attorney and to this day I have no idea how my name was on his mailing list.

I always felt that an elder care attorney should have someone in their office to help seniors—so I promptly called the law firm and asked to speak to Mr. Litherland, to ask if he had any office space. To my surprise he took the call and when I explained what I wanted to do, he suggested that I attend a seminar he was giving that day—in two hours to be exact—and we would talk later. We are still talking and continue to help our senior community in every way possible. I cannot thank Roy Litherland enough for taking that "leap of faith" allowing me to be an advisor to seniors and educating me in the law relating to seniors issues. It is with his guidance that we have achieved success in helping hundreds of families and seniors not only relating to the law but in all areas of daily life. Working and getting to know the seniors and their families inspired me to write this book. Hopefully, a word or a story will encourage another word or story helping seniors and families make decisions for today, tomorrow and beyond. Not to be forgotten a huge thank you to the staff of the law firm for there support throughout this journey.

I also want to thank Roy for agreeing to write the chapter on Legal Issues. His many years of experience has been invaluable to me and I hope his chapter will be as valuable to you as well. Thank you Roy, I owe you a huge debt of gratitude for giving me the opportunity to do what I truly wanted to do, help seniors and their families.

Jimmie Young of Tolman Creek Design deserves a major thank you for guiding me and gently critiquing my writing and offering consistent encouragement. His guidance has been immeasurable and I cannot imagine what I would have done without his suggestions, patience and unending guidance. Thank you to Shan Young for her editing skills and patience. What a comfort it is to know that Shan is there to make sure everything is done correctly. Holly Kennedy has done an amazing job designing my website and I am so grateful. Thank you Holly for what I had imagined to be so difficult, so enjoyable.

Finally, I want to thank Dr. Hardin Coleman, Dean and Professor of Counseling, Psychology and Human Development of Boston University for his generosity in writing such a sincere and generous "Forward". It means so very much to me.

Contents

FOREWORD

Lois Tager has written a timely and important book. Whether you are moving out of the home in which you have lived for many years, helping your parents move, or considering how you want to share your possessions with family members, this book has something for you. In addition to be written in a warm and graceful manner, it is filled with helpful suggestion about how to plan a move and, most important, how to deal with all the emotions that get aroused as you move and share your possessions. There is nothing easy about making these decisions and particularly if you are doing so in a crisis. This book is filled with helpful ideas about how to manage the stress and relationships. I particularly appreciated the many examples that Lois gives of how others have managed this situation. Lois does an excellent job of showing that there are many different ways to handle a situation and that it is important to pick the solution that is best for you. One issue that she presents very well is the issue of fairness. So many families struggle with trying to think about what is fair to everyone. Lois shows how hard that is to do, but that addressing this challenge systematically and with honesty is so often the best approach.

This book is authentic and useful. I strongly recommend that it be read by seniors and their children, close relationships, and friends. We all have a lot to learn from Lois' wisdom and warmth.

Hardin L.K. Coleman, Ph.D

Dean and Professor of Counseling, Psychology and Human Development of Boston University

BU School of Education

"Your Decisions, Your Stuff"

E ver since I was a child, my grandmother told me that someday, her engagement ring would be mine. I was named after her *mother* and because of that, she wanted me to have her ring. I never knew what the connection was between this beautiful ring and her *mother*. Now that I am writing this, I realize I should have asked. However, it was clear to my family that the ring would be mine. This ring became an important part of our family story. My grandmother had nine heart attacks. Every time she had "one" she would give me the ring. I, in turn quickly gave it back, knowing she would get better. When she was 83 years old she had a serious heart attack. I rushed to the hospital, nine months pregnant with my first child, to find her buried under an oxygen tent and very ill. As I approached her bedside and whispered hello to her, she quickly took off her ring and put it on my finger. I was not ready to see this wonderful woman who I dearly loved go; so I quickly told her "You can't go now because I am having my very first baby and I need you to be here when the baby is born." In a flash, she looked up at me and said, "You are absolutely right. I need to be here for that baby". With that said, I put the ring back on her finger. Three weeks later, my wonderful, beautiful grandmother was at my first child's baby naming ceremony, with her ring proudly on her finger. Five years later, after being there for each of my children, my "nanny" passed away. At that time, and almost 40 years later, her ring remains with me. I had her stones put into my wedding ring; therefore, I know she walks beside me each and every day.

This book is designed for all of us who have stories to tell and who have accumulated possessions—big and small, expensive or not—the treasures that make you smile, and perhaps one or two that do not. The purpose is to encourage and guide you through the process of making decisions regarding your "stuff", how to go about making those decisions, and why they are so very important.

In preparing for this book I sent out surveys to a number of people, and along with my questions and their answers, I asked if anyone had a story to share. Promising to refrain from using names, I also asked that I be allowed to share some of those beautiful stories. Throughout the book you will be reading some of these inspiring words.

Working with families over the years, I have witnessed moments of such strife and turmoil after a parent passes away, leaving the adult children to divide the estate's possessions and clean out the family home without the guidance of the beloved parent. The division and trauma that occurs within the family is often irreparable for many years. The purpose of this book is to hopefully protect some of us from the unnecessary trauma that would fracture a family forever.

I hope you enjoy this journey with me and learn how to avoid these unpleasantries in your family. This book will bring a smile and an occasional tear when you hear stories and solutions. The workbook or Journal provided will start you to think about your decisions and "what to do with your stuff".

Heirlooms and keepsakes in need of consideration.

PART I
DECISIONS

Family

CHAPTER ONE

WHY YOUR DECISIONS ARE IMPORTANT

I am writing this story because I realize how very important it is to share the special things in your life with the people you choose. Is there a special story that attaches to a favorite piece of jewelry, or a loving collectible such as an elephant or Hummel? Or perhaps you have a favorite pin, not necessarily an expensive one, but one that holds special meaning that you would like a daughter, daughter-in-law, grandchild, or friend to have as a remembrance. Have you told anyone the story behind that special ring, necklace, cake plate, cookie jar, golf club, or fishing pole?

This book is for you. It's purpose is to help you decide who you would like to receive your "stuff". Since I work with seniors as an advisor and geriatric care manager on a daily basis I often hear, "Let the kids decide who gets what". Do not put that burden on your children or loved ones. The simple act of not deciding for yourself and leaving it up to members of your family can cause difficulties beyond repair. What if after you're gone, your son decides to give an

A grandfather showing his grandchild a special fishing rod.

inexpensive ring to his wife when your daughter (his sister) wanted it to be hers? I have seen something so simple destroy relationships between siblings and other family members. Do not let that happen to your family.

I am often asked "what exactly is a geriatric care manager? The National Association of Professional Geriatric Care Managers defines the profession as follows:

"A professional Geriatric Care Manager (GCM) is a health and human services specialist who helps families who are caring for older relatives. The GCM is trained and experienced in any of several fields related to care management, including nursing, gerontology, social work, or psychology."

Geriatric Care Managers and Certified Senior Advisors have vast knowledge regarding aging and issues affecting the elderly. We help seniors and their families in various ways that enable them to make informed decisions with a higher level of confidence as we offer credible sources of contacts, resources and information. We are able to make assessments both in the home or in the hospital environment to offer advice and direction. We develop care plans and make recommendations to help seniors' age within their own home. Through our assessment, recommendations are made and a plan is developed. If there is a need to leave the home, we help educate and introduce seniors to the many types of communities available. Geriatric Care Managers visit facilities and evaluate their strengths and weaknesses. We are there to advocate for the senior in whatever circumstance presents itself. We offer assistance to our clients through a wide variety of resources, knowledge and expertise.

As part of a law firm, we are unique and knowledgeable regarding senior services as well as the law as it pertains to seniors and work closely with our attorneys' on the senior's behalf.

Jayne writes: "I think it would be great to have a step by step list of things one needs to do as one gets to various stages of less independence to eliminate as much as possible to avoid burdening someone else be it children, grandchildren, spouse, etc. A checklist of sorts to make things as easy as possible and to take much guess work as possible out of the process".

Deciding who gets what can be easy and at the same time difficult. You may decide on what one person gets, but not know what others will want or appreciate. If you are someone who collects "things" because they mean something special to you, now is the time to record the person who is connected to this item and the story about it that you wish to share. Perhaps you purchased a candy dish while shopping with friends and it is simply a memory of that day or those friends. Our "stuff" may be an inexpensive trinket or an expensive diamond pendant. It may be a single, special golf club when you finally scored that hole in one, or an old, used and worn watch that your grandson played with when he was a baby. It is special to you— perhaps it will be special to someone you choose to own it. It is your choice. Telling your story about that special something gives it life, a part of your life, and therefore it becomes more meaningful. Dr. Bill Thomas writes in *Second Wind* "the life story of an elder rightly understood offers us the distilled essence of life as one human being has lived it. All of the great story listeners in history have understood that opening one's mind can change a

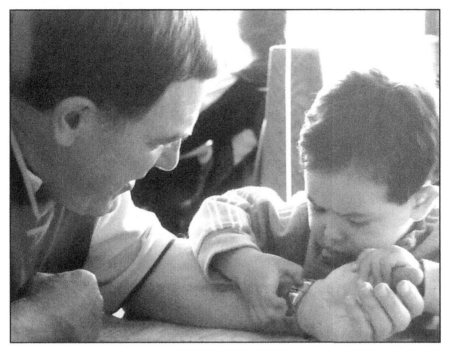

Grandson playing with grandfather's watch.

familiar tale into something new, something that can change how we see the world."

Recently, a lovely "young" woman of 88, Edna, told me "she woke up one day and called her four daughters to come to her home on Sunday, no spouses or children. They were only told that it was important. When the "girls" arrived, she had placed her precious keepsakes, jewelry, figurines, etc., on the dining room table, she then explained that she wanted them to choose what they wanted. However, the one thing she would not tolerate is anyone arguing over a particular piece. If that happened, she would put it aside and decide later who would be the one to get it, and they would find out about it after she was gone. Edna was delighted that the day went well. With any items left over, she wrote a list and made the final decisions as to who gets what.

In this particular instance, her daughters were able to get along quite well. This does not work for all families. Edna did not have daughters-in-law. Would she have included them if she did? Too often I hear, "I am not giving my "good" things to my daughters-in-law; after all, what if there is a divorce, or my daughter-in-law and I don't particularly get along." Or most common "my daughter-in-law will get her Mother's things." This is a very personal decision. I have heard many stories about daughters-in-law, and in many cases the relationship is not always cohesive. I am very fortunate to have wonderful daughters-in-law who I highly respect and admire. I am grateful that they are wonderful wives to my sons and great mothers to my grandchildren. So for me, I do not have a problem leaving something special to my daughters-in-law. I do hope that if there ever were to be a change in the marital relationship, they would pass the inherited item to their daughters and/or sons. Try to include each one of your daughters, sons, daughters-in-law, sons-in-law and grandchildren when selecting who gets what. Leaving something to someone often leaves a soft, sweet feeling in the recipient.

Speaking of sons and grandsons, I was recently reminded that sons and grandsons also really appreciate having something special from their grandparents. Women often think of what should I leave my "girls", thinking that their "men" would never want any of the "stuff". Not so, often the men/boys feel left out and a bit saddened that they were not included. Dads and grandfathers, perhaps you have a special watch, or firearm, or golf club, or fishing gear that you would like your sons or grandsons to own. Sons and grandsons will cherish something from Mom as well, perhaps the special candy dish that was always there when the children came home from school.

Recently a special client, Gus, came to see me with a "dilemma". He wanted to leave a piece of property to his grandson who he dearly loved. We shall call his grandson "Nick". He had a number of grandchildren, both male and female, but he was closest to Nick. In many respects, Nick had become his caretaker, always checking up on this 88 year old, dropping in to visit Gus during the week and weekends, stopping by to pick him up for lunch, helping with his home and chores, taking him shopping, and never once had the grandfather asked him to do it. He felt there was a special bond between the two of them. When writing an amendment to his trust, he decided to leave the piece of land to his grandson. He was in a position to leave a substantial amount of money to the rest of his sons and grandchildren. He decided to tell Nick's father, his son, that he was leaving the land to Nick. His son became enraged. He wanted the land. His son, however, hardly saw his Dad, rarely visited, was always too busy to spend any time visiting, or helping this elderly gentleman. The final decision belonged to Gus.

Making your own decisions regarding your possessions and your life choices regarding end of life, will unburden your family from making decisions at an emotional and distressing time.

According to the *"The Story of Stuff Project"*, statistics on "stuff" tell us that the average person's consumption in the United States is twice what it was 50 years ago.

We collect more "must haves" than any previous generation. It brings pleasure for the moment, and then we place the item on a shelf and eventually forget that item that we first could not live without. You use or enjoy today perhaps 10% of all your "must haves".

The purpose of this book is not to address Hoarding. There is a distinct difference between pack rats and hoarders and those of us who are collectors. Professor Randy O. Frost, a professor of psychology at Smith College and author of *Stuff: Compulsive Hoarding and The Meaning Of Things*, says that "the difference is in how the collection is stored and organized." The hoarder is one "whose possessions become unorganized piles of clutter that are so large that they prevent rooms from being used for normal activities." In my experience, hoarders have piles of stuff as well as boxes and boxes, often preventing one from walking safely through their home.

Those of us, who are collectors, have curios and cabinets that hold our treasures. However, what will happen to all those "treasures" when we are no longer able to enjoy them? Recently, Angela Hill of the *Mercury News* wrote about a young woman who had to sort through her late mother's garage. "Her mother was sentimental and she kept everything, even some antiques such as vintage milk glass. She also saved 60 years worth of Christmas cards and multitudes of similar things. It was a huge challenge to purge, recycle, and donate as much as possible. " The young woman reported that, "her mother's accumulation was overwhelming and mind-numbing."

Making your own decisions as to who gets what of your collections, treasures, and stuff is a gift to your children, family and friends.

In my practice, I am presented with many seniors as the one I just described. This is the reason for writing this book. To encourage you to "decide who gets what" and take the burden away from your family after you are gone. In the following chapters, you will find many ideas as to how to do this, the why, and for who is up to you.

Are you beginning to think of which one of your special possessions you would like to give to someone in particular? A Journal has been provided for you at the back of the book. This will be your own very personal journal for you to record your stories and preferences. Let's get started!

Your choice, your wishes...

Why A Story

When you were a child, did you want something so badly but was told, "so sorry but it is too expensive" we just cannot afford to buy that shinny red car or special baby doll? Months later your birthday, Christmas, or a special occasion happened, and you were surprised with that shinny red car or special baby doll. What a wonderful feeling receiving something so special.

Growing up your Mom always made her very own recipe for sweet potato pie for thanksgiving that everyone loved or the chocolate chip coffee cake that was the most delicious cake you had ever eaten. You have such fond memories of that sweet potato pie and that coffee cake, how wonderful it would be to have that cake recipe and pie plate and the stories of those special moments. The stories help to enhance the memories and keep them alive.

On one very beautiful spring day I met my husband for lunch in our usual spot near his office. I had been ill and it felt so good to be able to be out and about. As we were leaving the restaurant, my husband suggested we stop at our jeweler's to pick up his watch, which had been repaired. We walked into the jewelers, and as he was getting his watch I wandered around the store admiring so many beautiful "trinkets" as he often called them. The jeweler, Dave, walked up to me and said, "Why don't you try on the necklace you were admiring". I protested and he explained that it was new and he wanted to see how it looked. So I agreed and he placed this beautiful necklace on my neck. With my husband watching, he then announced, "This is for you. Happy Mother's Day"! My husband had arranged this amazing surprise. Every time I look at this necklace, I think of that special moment and it warms my heart with a smile.

Sharing your special stories give your "stuff" more value. Value is not what it costs, but what it means to you. This is the Value of the Heart. Memories that stay alive in the ones we love. When an adult child holds something dear from a parent, the essence of that parent lives on. Special family belongings serve as a connection to the past. No matter what the origin, whether they are from family members who arrived from another country, or those too old to tell, their connection to you and your family remains and is a connection to past loved ones.

Many objects tell a story of family events and memories of those special moments such as a wedding, baptism, thanksgiving, or Christmas dinner. Telling stories helps family members connect to generations past and they learn to appreciate survival and accomplishments. These stories help to preserve family history, life's special moments, and traditions, for past, present, and future generations.

Telling the story is a wonderful thing for you and your loved ones, but writing your story in your own words, stays forever. If writing is too difficult, have a family member video your stories or use a tape recorder.

What is your special story? Take a moment and go to the Journal at the back of this book and start writing, or just make some notes to remind you that you have a story that you wish to share.

A very beautiful sample story:

Diane Nichols story: *Precious Pearls*

"Ever since I was a little girl, my grandmother spoke of the very special pearls that had been in her family for generations. 'One day they will be yours to pass down to your daughter or granddaughter,' she'd say—but I never actually saw the legendary necklace.

"When Gran was 89, she left this earth, leaving a deep void in my heart. As we packed up her tiny bedroom, I found a jewelry box containing only a few costume pieces and an old brooch, and I immediately worried that something had happened to Gran's cherished pearls.

"To my surprise, though, at the bottom of the box was a worn leather journal, and on the cover was a sticky note with my name on it. My eyes filled with tears as I read the words 'Pearls of Wisdom' on the first page.

Written by Gran's grandmother, her mother, then Gran herself were pages full of funny and powerful nuggets like: 'Always sing in the shower,' 'Lick the beaters' and 'Don't fall in love, leap into it.' As it turns our, Gran's pearls' were more beautiful and precious than I ever imagined."

A grandmother and her grandchild.

CHAPTER TWO

THE ART OF MAKING DECISIONS

M aking decisions for many of us does not come easily and for others, quite easily.

Why can some people discard everything, magazines, coupons, clothes and more and others continue to collect and keep life's accumulations, unable to part with any of it. Others may want to make the change but do not have any idea as to how or where to begin.

Whether you part with everything and then regret it or keep every outfit you have had for 20 years, know that you are not alone. Doctors, lawyers, nurses, professionals, successful business owners, homemakers all share the problem of keeping too much stuff. Many are organized at work but their homes are cluttered with books, magazines and additional materials they are unable to part with. Linda Anderson, MA, MCC, SCAC in her article *Why Is it So Hard To Let Go Of All That Stuff* outlines a number of categories of collectors and clutterers. Perhaps you will find one of these categories which describes your dilemma in getting rid of your stuff or will help you when deciding it is time.

The first category is the environmentalists. These individuals cannot bear to part with anything regarding "waste to our planet" or "something they will be able to reuse". Therefore they find a use for almost everything.

Anderson's second category she calls the "paper mystic, one who finds giving up printed material impossible, because every word and every page holds potential meaning in their life." They are unable to throw out stacks of unread material whether they are magazines, newspapers, books or journals fearing that someday they will need to find the answers to questions pertaining to life.

The "archivist feels a religious attachment to anything old". Holding onto letters, old photos and trinkets bring back memories of the past , which they too often talk about and cling to. They would rather refer to the past then make decisions regarding the future.

The touchy-feely person is sentimental and collects items which conjure up special memories and often carry a story along with it. They are more comfortable surrounded by stuff they can feel and see.

The next category is the "artisan". The artisan is one who keeps about everything feeling that one day they would be able to turn the article into a piece of sculpture or perhaps a lovely pillow or simple mobile. They keep scraps of cloth, holiday decorations from many years past and various objects.

The "Perfectionist is one who hides out under paper and old stuff". "They won't even get started on clearing out the clutter, because they can not do it perfectly."

The last of Anderson's categories is the "procrastinator. This is someone who avoids the task of decluttering or who appears to avoid it." "They share some of the characteristics of previous categories." Perhaps they never learned how to be organized, make decisions easily and avoid change. Therefore, they choose not to do anything and often need encouragement and help to make decisions and change.

Recently I visited a friend and noticed that she did not have one single thing out of place, no trinkets displayed and not a single piece of paper. When I mentioned that I was a bit envious that she was able to keep everything emaculate and did not see a single piece of paper, she confessed to me that she throws out everything. Every six months she cleans out her closet and gives to charity all clothes she has not worn in the past six months. On occasion she is sorry she discards everything so quickly and has thrown out paperwork she needed and must recreate and clothing she should never have given away. Perhaps we should add a category for the compulsive discarder.

While reading the list of categories, I found myself chuckling when I realized that I am somewhat a touchy-feely person. I enjoy reminiscing about past pleasures when I see some of my stuff in the curio and often have stories as well. Do you find that you recognize some of your traits in one of these categories? I do believe that we all have some traits that we would like to see changed and others that are just fine. Step one to letting go of your stuff is recognizing why you may not want to let special items go and feel you need help in deciding where, when and to whom.

Letting go of our stuff is often very emotional. Perhaps you were given a piece of jewelry given to you by your parent who received it from their parent. Making the decision as to who will be the next in line to receive this lovely bracelet may be difficult. There should be no doubt that when you are no longer around, your decision as to who shall receive this heirloom has been made by you and is carefully written along with its historical story.

While traveling, you purchased a small replica of the very first cruise you took, a beautiful small sailboat. When looking at that sailboat today, it stirs your emotions as you recall the romantic nights, exciting places you visited and how special you felt surrounded by love and tranquility. Close your eyes and you can still remember the water lapping at the boat, snuggled in your tiny stateroom experiencing feelings of contentment. When you are asked to "get rid of your stuff", emotional jitters can override reason as you look around your home.

I approached a lovely, small English Tudor style, two-story home surrounded by ivy. Although the grounds were slightly overgrown and the paint was in need of repair, I could imagine the pride of ownership this home had once enjoyed. An old antique wheel barrel adorned the front garden with marigolds peeking out from the weathered greens. Mr. and Mrs. Chen had lived in this home for 50 years where they raised their four sons. Mrs. Chen was not well and could no longer take care of her home. Their children were off in different directions creating their own lives and careers. Mr. Chen knew that they must move into a smaller, more manageable home but was overcome with fear and sadness. His wife loved her antiques and books she had gathered over the years. Their sons were encouraging them to "get rid of the stuff" and move. Mrs. Chen looked at her beautiful antiques, which had the power to unlock the most emotional memories of shopping for and choosing just the right antique set of teacups she proudly displayed in her curio cabinet. The master bedroom on the second floor was just too difficult to navigate more than once a day. Intellectually they knew that it was time to think about moving but emotionally they were overwhelmed. It was extremely difficult to decide what to take with them and what to part with. Even though the neighborhood was changing with younger families moving in, they were afraid to leave. During a recent snowstorm, the new young couple across the street had shoveled out the snow from their back door so they could get out if necessary and even offered to go to the market to purchase milk and bread or anything else they might need

Mr. Chen was concerned about the cost of a new home. And what would happen if they moved and did not like it? They would not have their home to return to. If they did decide to move, how were they to dispose of the possessions they decided not to take? Their sons could choose what ever they wanted but what about the rest of their stuff? Would they sell it? Donate it? They felt there was so much to think about. Their children agreed to help them with every step of the move assuring them that they would not have to do it alone.

Finances

Frequently and of paramount importance in most everyone's life is the question "do I have enough money to retire and continue to live the lifestyle that I enjoy now". One of the biggest regrets of retirees is that they had not begun to save at a younger age. Many people were hurt by the 2008 recession and now must look at retirement differently. Seniors are choosing to stay in the workforce whether full time or part-time. The rising cost of goods and services has had a direct effect on our retirement dollars. Due to the wonders of medicine, our senior population especially our oldest, old (over 85) are living significantly longer. More than a third of retirees with children and grandchildren are contributing to their support as well as taking care of aging parents. Therefore, retirement for some has been delayed due to family obligations. Those that can retire, are wisely seeking advice from financial experts who can try to project how much money is needed to maintain a comparable lifestyle.

"Families that learn to talk to one another candidly about sensitive topics will thrive. So will people who see retirement as a glorious mixture of work, play and learning. After all, growing old can be viewed as a kind of second adolescence. Like the first one, it is fraught with exhilaration and fear of the unknown. The difference is that this time you are bringing wisdom with you. Thus the experience should be that much sweeter." *Living Well in Retirement* by Lisa Ellis and the editors of *Money* magazine.

Shortly after her father passed away. Allison's mother gave her home to her only child, and her husband David. She remained with them for another ten years until she passed. The home was on an acre of land, which David continued to mow, prune trees and shrubs and take care of all the demands of a large property. The home had three stories needing many repairs. The Lang's had lived in the home for 35 years and were exhausted by the upkeep. The home was located quite a distance from town and required them to drive wherever they needed to go whether it was for shopping, doctor visits and entertainment. David recently learned about an adult community, which offered activities such as golf, which he loved, tennis and much more. The Lang's decided to visit the new community to learn more about it and consider whether a move to a senior community would work for them. The following week David and Allison visited the "Woodlands". Taking a tour of the grounds and residences, the community seemed very friendly, was located near a college which invited seniors to take classes for reduced rates. It offered a special program for seniors to hear visiting professors lecture on various subjects, such as travel programs and offered one the opportunity to obtain degrees if one wanted to pursue that avenue. They talked to the tour guide of the Woodlands about availability and types of residences, the cost of ownership, the homeowners' fees, golf membership, and any other fees to be aware of.

As they were returning home there was silence in the car as each of them considered all that they had learned. Allison kept thinking of the beautiful homes. She certainly would not mind taking care of a smaller home and everything was so new and fresh. She loved the idea that the clubhouse offered a swimming pool and art classes, which she had always wanted to try. David was picturing the beautiful golf course, which he could play at any time he chose, and all the amenities the Woodlands offered. At the same time, he was worried whether they could afford to live in such a lifestyle. Would they be able to sell their home for a reasonable price? Would their savings support them for many years to come in such a community? Almost simultaneously, they both started talking about could they make it work. David and Allison decided that the next step would be to seek council from their accountant and financial advisor .

The financial advisor developed long-range projections demonstrating that, if they invested conservatively, they would have enough money to live comfortably in such a senior community. Their accountant concurred with the financial advisor. They met with a realtor to get an estimate of their property's current value. They would then be able to make an educated decision.

Change

Change is intrinsic to every one of us from the moment of birth. We are constantly changing when we make something different. Change occurs daily with the weather and leaves changing color in the fall. We change from something small to something larger. Change is also motivated by choice and we, as thinking and doing individuals, make choices to change or not. Simple changes like changing from work clothes to play clothes or old curtains to new curtains may take a small amount of effort. Greater changes may be to change jobs for something that we perceive to be better paying or a more pleasant arena in which to work. Changing one's living environment is to enter into something new and different. We can always find the negatives and positives in any new situation. When we are young, starting something new is exciting and invigorating. When we are older, we resist starting something new and different and often fail to see that change will open up new avenues and positive experiences.

Evelyn and Peter Benson have lived in California for 48 years. They moved to the west coast when Peter was transferred from upstate New York. They had two children, a daughter, Grace, now married with four beautiful grandchildren, lived in Colorado. Their son, Tim and his wife lived in Arizona. Evelyn and Peter were approaching there 80's and were not in the best of health. Their children were constantly encouraging them to sell their home and move closer to them. The children, concerned that something drastic might happen to their parents, wanted their parents to move closer to family.

Although they had a modest home in a nice neighborhood, it was getting more difficult to take care of everything both inside and out. Many of their friends had moved closer to their children but they still had a number of very close friends that they loved dearly and hated to leave.

Evelyn and Peter were somewhat set in their ways and never liked change. That was one of the reasons they remained in their small home, drove an eleven-year-old car and often talked about what was rather than what will be. However, they were lonely and missed their children and grandchildren. They kept reminding each other that they were missing the kid's important moments such as birthdays and anniversaries. If they moved, difficult as that might be, their lives would be enriched by family, living close by and learning about their new environment.

They would be able to attend their grandchildren's school plays, music recitals and soccer games. They especially would not have to worry about where to turn to if they became ill. They decided to focus on all the positives. It would make the move much easier.

To accomplish this move, outside help would be necessary. With the decision made, they hired a relocation company to facilitate the move. Evelyn and Peter found themselves actually looking forward to their new adventure.

Health

Staying healthy and feeling our best at every age is important. However, health certainly does play a part in our decisions regarding how we live our lives. Can and do we exercise such as walking, bike riding, exercising in the gym or running on a treadmill? Health often affects career changes. Do we retire because of our health or return to work because we feel well enough to do so? Often we hear that healthy changes such as reinventing yourself to pass through the aging cycle such as doing work that you always wanted to do, starting something entirely new and staying socially active are extremely important and can contribute to maintaining good health.

How many times have you heard "laughter is the best medicine"? Laughter is truly the stabilizer and the key to relaxing mind and body. Do not underestimate the importance of reading and exercises for your mind, Sudoku, crossword puzzles and the like stimulate the mind. Staying socially active with friends and family also contribute to better health and well-being. Often I hear a client say "I just do not know what to do with myself" and we explore their likes and dislikes. How about volunteering? Every community has organizations that depend on and desperately need volunteers. Hospitals use volunteers for many things such as greeting visitors, delivering newspapers and a myriad list of other necessary functions. Some hospitals have volunteers helping in the infant and children's department for those children needing more attention. The Alzheimer's association actively solicits volunteers to help with call lines and facilitating caregiver groups. Libraries look for volunteers to help assist in teaching adults to read. Most volunteer positions offer training programs and appreciate your time whether it is one hour a week or once a month. Keeping busy whether volunteering or socializing contributes to better health and peace of mind.

A 76-year-old gentleman came to see me about his wife who had Alzheimer's and was living in a facility. He visited her daily, however, after his visit with his wife he felt lost and lonely. During our discussion he mentioned that although he was an engineer for his entire adult life, he always wanted to be a doctor. We talked about the possibility of volunteering at a local hospital. The very next day he called the hospital to see if he could volunteer and was quickly welcomed into the hospital's volunteer organization. Three times a week he volunteers for three hours greeting visitors. He continues to visit his wife but now has an entire new group of volunteer friends. Volunteering gave this gentleman a purpose in life allowing him to feel needed and rejuvenated.

Caregivers struggle with caring for their loved ones and caring for themselves. The loving relationship a wife has with her husband or that of the husband caring for his wife is often strained and reversed when one is suffering from an illness and the other becomes the caregiver. The roles of their relationship often shift and often become strained. The needs of the caregiver must be considered to help maintain a loving relationship within the confines of the illness. When a loved one, be it spouse, mother, father or special needs child needing twenty-four seven care, additional help must be available to help the caregiver.

Relationships

Much has been written about relationships between older adults. Interviews conducted by Reichstadt et al (2010) note that those who found a meaningful way to stay active in society by working, volunteering or interacting socially expressed a greater source of happiness. *Relationships Among the Elderly: The Effects on One's Health and Psychosocial Well Being "Abstract"* Journal of Nursing.

Relationships vary regardless of age and are guided by the personalities of the seniors' lifestyles, fulfillment levels and adaptation to the aging process. Relationships differ whether they are marital, family or social. Often, the seniors' quality of life contributes to how they view their relationships. If one is involved with their family in a positive way, they tend not to feel so isolated and lonely. Seniors especially respond positively when they know someone cares about them. Caring can provide a sense of well being.

A curio cabinet of treasures.

CHAPTER THREE

AVOIDING AVOIDANCE

Deciding who gets what places the decision in your hands and eliminates potential problems later on. I often hear clients tell me, "Not a problem, my kids can figure it out after I am gone."

That works, some of the time. However, most of the time, in my experience, it does not work at all. One sibling always wants something the other one desires.

"Edna always placed a small candy dish in the front hall so when the children came home from school, they had a candy treat." Edna passed away and never thought to leave that candy dish to any one in particular. She never thought that anyone would want that "old thing". It wasn't particularly pretty or special in any way. That, however, was not how her children viewed the dish. They both wanted that candy dish because of the memories it brought with it. They argued and became very testy toward each other—over this tiny candy dish. When they came to see me, sitting on opposite sides of the room, I heard their side of the argument. The son felt he wanted it because he had young children and he could provide the same type of loving memories for them—leaving candy to his children. The daughter wanted it for sentimental reasons and could not understand why her brother even cared. It was causing great discord between the two. The end result—they shared the dish— one keeping it six months of the year and then giving it to the other for six months. They agreed on the arrangements and immediately started to rebuild their discordant relationship—all this over a candy dish.

By making a list of who is to receive your favorite paintings, dishes, collectibles, furniture, or antique cars, you are telling your family that these are your wishes—your choice.

Eileen wrote: "My paternal Grandmother was a very important part of our family. My father died when I was six years old and his mother and stepfather were a tremendous help to my mother who was a 33 year old widow with three young kids. As I grew up, I admired my grandmother for her strength and tenacity. My family was not wealthy, however, my grandmother had accumulated a sizeable estate towards the end of her life. She was very organized and practical and had decided that she would put stickers, i.e., labels with the name of the person who would receive a painting, lamp, etc., after her death. Before my grandfather passed away, they moved into an assisted living facility. My grandmother gave heirloom pieces of furniture to the three grandchildren. When my grandfather died, my grandmother naturally became very emotional and unusually attached to her possessions. She repeatedly changed the names on the back of mirrors, paintings, china, etc. which had been previously designated to another sibling. At one point it became a little morbid and comical in our family. Although we thought we knew what we were originally "bequeathed", at the end of her life, it was all mixed up and my siblings and I didn't know what we were receiving and it put an unnecessary burden on us."

Putting your wishes in writing often helps to avoid complications such as the one above. If Eileen's grandmother decided to make changes, that would have been fine, and writing it would have been much more definitive for her grandchildren.

Tagore once wrote, "The depth of a friendship does not depend on the length of an acquaintance".

In thinking about whom you would like to choose for certain items, remember to think about close friends as well. In many families, close friends are part of the family. If you do not have a family member to leave something to, think of your dear friends. You may have friends from many years past or newer friends that have become very important and precious. Have you every thought about leaving something to a close friend? If not, you may want to consider this as a possibility.

What is Fair?

Often the subject comes up as to choosing one person or another and being fair when deciding who gets what. For many, being fair is extremely important. What exactly does fairness mean to you? Should one divide everything equally? How can that be done when one treasure may mean more emotionally but is of lesser value than another? Being fair to all members of the family is important but not usually practical. If one member of the family has a greater need than another, do we leave more to the needy one hoping that the rest of the family will understand?

Fair does not always mean equal. In years past, it was customary to leave the oldest son the family property. As time went on, this custom was replaced by leaving everything equally, but only to blood relatives, therefore eliminating in-laws and friends. Do we leave an expensive piece of jewelry to one child and therefore try to match the value and number of items given to another child? If one is in great need and the others are highly successful, do we choose to give only to the child in need?

Many people believe that using a fair process is more important than actually who gets what. When in doubt, approaching the family and presenting the question "what is fair" will certainly help to determine what the family is thinking.

"My parents recently died within three months of each other. My sister, brother and I have been going through the house and making decisions about who gets what. It's gone pretty smoothly. There is one item in the whole house that all three of us really want—the *Winnie the Pooh* book that Mom and Dad read to each of us when we were young. It has always been kept in the corner bookshelf in the living room. There is simply no way to divide the book equally among the three of us. We've considered each having it for a year and rotating possessions, but that seems really tedious over time." Marlene E. Stum, Ph. D, *The Fairness Issue in Estate Planning*, CSA Journal, No 53 2013.

In such cases, families often equalize the situation by drawing names or numbers, drawing straws or any number of ways to determine who should receive the item. If you recall, earlier I mentioned the situation with the candy dish that almost brought brother and sister to such a conflicted state, they needed a mediator to resolve the issue.

We must realize that there is no right answer. Fairness is not a "one size fits all" consideration. What is fair when one is making financial decisions will differ from what is fair regarding caregiving roles. Ultimately the decision lies with the one making the gift. In families that are cantankerous, decisions made regarding important holdings such as land and costly valuables should be recorded in one's Trust and/or Will.

Downsizing

Let's talk a moment about the word "Downsizing". When I hear the word it usually refers to companies downsizing, and eventually people loosing their jobs. In my experience, seniors often resist downsizing, thinking that they are showing a weakness, or that their life is slowing down. I think it is time for seniors to look at downsizing as a good thing. From now on I will refer to it as Revitalizing.

When I moved from a large home to one half the size, I had no idea as to what we would do with all the furniture, paintings, and collectibles. However, we were doing this to take care of a family member and so I rationalized that it was not a bad thing to do. What I learned is that it is truly revitalizing to your lifestyle and your health. No longer do I worry about the care of a large home when taking care of the smaller home is much easier, requires much less time, and allows me to do the things I often felt I did not have time to do. We can make any situation work if we believe it will work. So if you find yourself needing to change living arrangements, do so with a positive attitude that it will be better for you, and allow you new opportunities to experience and enjoy. If you choose to move to a new community, then you have opportunities to meet new friends and participate in new activities. It can be enlightening and joyful.

Are you unsure about what type of home you would consider? Here is some basic information on the different types of senior living communities and some questions to ask when thinking of revitalizing.

Independent Living is ideal for someone who is independent, self-sufficient and relatively healthy. You may still be driving or not, do not mind preparing a meal or two but would rather not, and are tired of caring for your home, the gardens and all the responsibility that living in one's home requires. Independent living can be a separate small unit in a retirement community, attached townhouse or condo apartment. Most independent living facilities offer at least one meal a day, and some offer more. More often than not, homes and apartments are designed for easy maintenance and the utmost safety of their inhabitants. Additionally, seniors living in this type of housing usually have easy access to health services and other amenities such as social activities.

Board and Care homes are smaller, privately owned homes assisting individuals with grooming, bathing, meal preparation and medical management. In most instances, board and care homes have approximately six residents and two caregivers. Some do offer activities and field trips. Be sure to inquire as to exactly what the planned activities are for a day when seeking out information. Some offer transportation to medical offices most, however, rely on families for medical appointments and off campus excursions.

Assisted living is an option for those seniors who cannot live entirely on their own. Assisted living is designed for those suffering from mild to moderate health conditions, as well as requiring additional care and medication management. Assistance is provided for those residents who may need additional care in dressing, bathing and grooming. Three meals a day are provided and social activities are offered daily. In many assisted living communities, transportation is provided to shopping centers, medical appointments and entertainment.

Skilled nursing care is available for those seniors who are suffering from severe medical conditions and require 24-hour medical care in all activities of daily living, such as bathing, dressing, assistance walking or wheelchair bound, as well as personal care and grooming. All meals are included and physical and occupational rehabilitation therapy is available to patients.

If you have a loved one with Alzheimer's and are considering a facility specifically for that purpose, be sure to learn about the caregiver to patient ratio. In fact, I believe that is a question one should ask in skilled nursing homes as well. It is suggested that 1 caregiver to 8 patients is acceptable and in an Alzheimer's facility the ratio should be considerably less. Be sure to inquire as to staff availability in the evening and during the night.

When visiting various properties, ask if they offer transportation for medical appointments, shopping and outside activities. Be sure to inquire about hairdressing and barber facilities. Are your meal times flexable? For some this is extremely important as not everyone wishes to eat at the exact same time every day. Most facilities encourage their residents to attend social activities. We know that socialization for all seniors helps maintain mental acuity. Activities offer stimulation, physically as well as mentally.

Most important, keep in mind that in any facility, regardless of age or mental function, one needs an advocate asking the questions we do not think of when we are ill or infirmed or overwhelmed by new surroundings. Whether one is supporting a friend or relative, being there, showing love and understanding is a priceless gift.

As you consider your downsizing or revitalizing options, ask yourself questions such as:

1. What is most important to me in choosing where I live?
2. What do you enjoy? For example: would you like to be near the ocean or a golf course?
3. What do you want more of in your life?
4. What do you want less of in your life?
5. What gives you joy?
6. What is the cost, and am I able to afford the change in financial circumstances?

Visit different facilities for "over 55" and see what appeals to you the most. If you are not sure moving into a new facility is affordable be sure to contact your financial planners. If you need further assistance, contact geriatric care managers in your area for guidance. Geriatric care managers will consider all your health and physical needs and often will accompany you on tours as well.

Are you thinking of "revitalizing", perhaps to a smaller home or assisted living, and will not need many of your possessions? Making decisions when leaving your home is often monumental. How do I decide on what to keep and what to take? First, try to distinguish needs from wants. Think about what you will truly need in your new home. Perhaps this would be a good time to give some of your cherished possessions and keepsakes to a special person. Not only will it help you revitalize but you will receive the joy of giving and seeing that person enjoy your gift.

Moving to a smaller home usually does not allow you to take all your furniture. To help you decide what to take, make a floor plan of the new home, then decide what will work inside your new home before you move out of your old home. If you now have a sofa both in the family room and living room, and you can only use one sofa, choose the one that is the most comfortable. Prioritize what are the must have's and eliminate those that must go by either selling or donating to a local charity.

Have you started writing? It is never too early or too late to write your decisions!

CHAPTER FOUR

ONE ROOM AT A TIME... OR NOT

It takes a great deal of effort to contemplate going through your collections, jewelry, and all the special things one collects over the years. Many of us travel and often pick up souvenirs that remind us of wonderful moments and special people. Remember, the value is not necessarily what it costs but what it means to you.

Keep in mind that if a family member suffers from dementia, clutter poses a serious risk. As the disease advances these issues will only get worse, to ensure safety and accessibility the home environment should be clutter free.

The effort it takes just thinking about going through all our "stuff" is daunting and exhausting. We tend to put things off and hope that someone else will make the decision and do the work. Going though all our "stuff" might take days, weeks, or even longer.

"Procrastination is the thief of dreams". (Anonymous)

It is not as difficult as you may think and here are some simple suggestions. Start small with just one drawer, jewelry box, or a curio cabinet. If you are ready to tackle more then choose one corner of one room. Start with items that are easily accessible.

To begin, plan on working just one hour. This will make the project less daunting. Do not attempt to do everything at once. Spending one hour will not exhaust you emotionally or physically and will allow you to return again and again to the project.

Once you find a special item, write it down, then decide who will be the recipient and go onto the next item. To make this easier for you, a Journal is included in the back of this book.

It certainly will help to get you started. Describe the article. If you wish, write why it is special to you and who will receive it when you are no longer around. You may also share a story about it.

Or, you may wish to give that special figurine now, for a holiday, birthday gift, or just because you wish to see the joy when they receive it. Spending one hour at a time will not exhaust you emotionally or physically and will allow you to return often. When you have a sense of accomplishment, you will want to continue to do more.

A Story example: Linda writes: "My father set the bar for distribution. He had two daughters and two granddaughters. He went through some of his favorite pieces and placed a piece of masking tape with our names on the bottom of each piece. Upon his passing, it was a special gift to realize he had thought specifically about each of us. However, we also received some special pieces in my parent's lifetime. Rather than waiting until they passed, they gave us some collectibles beforehand and I loved that. I have started to do the same thing. I like seeing the joy it brings my daughter and the stories I can tell her about the piece I have given to her. Why wait?"

To make this process as easy as possible, you may wish to categorize your possessions into groups such as:

- Jewelry
- Collectables
- Serving Pieces
- China
- Furniture
- Male/Female items that do not fall into the above categories.
- Charatable Donations

Additionally, you may choose to label each item. However, if you think there is a possibility that someone might be "naughty" and switch the labels, then write your list in the Journal or set up a card file for each one of your treasures. If you choose to use a card file, include your stories on the card as well.

Another suggestion is to take a picture of each item. This is easily done with the new Polaroid cameras that comes with a small printer, allowing you to print the picture on an adhesive back paper. Place the picture in your book, marking it for whom it will be given; telling the story as well. Fuji has a similar product.

If you find this absolutely daunting and you are unable to do this alone, keep in mind that there are a number of professional "organizers" who, for a fee, will help you. Working with a specialist will help to guide you and help to accomplish your goals.

I recently had the privilege to speak with Michele Worthington and Elizabeth Obermeyer, long-time professional organizers located in San Francisco, CA. They offered some very helpful hints. Michele told the story of Aunt Gigi's towel. Aunt Gigi was a beloved aunt of a client of Michele's named Jill. Jill, as a child, often visited with Aunt Gigi who loved the color purple. Every thing in her home was purple, including her towels. When Aunt Gigi passed away, Jill took one of Aunt Gigi's towels as a remembrance of this wonderful woman. As the years passed the towel became less important and the memories more dear. When Michele was working with Jill, she asked Jill do you "love it or use it?" Jill smiled and said "no, she had not used it or even thought about it in years". Michele reminded Jill that the memories would always be there and the towel was no longer important. The towel was discarded. Having a professional organizer who is impartial often helps to make the process of deciding what to keep and what to discard much easier.

Elizabeth recommended that if you decide to hire an organizer but are not sure how much time you will need to use them, start with four hours if you have a great deal of "stuff". If that works well, you can always ask for more time. Going it alone can be difficult and having professional help will make it easier and less daunting. Organizers can help separate the emotion attached to the item.

To choose a professional to help you, contact the National Association of Professional Organizers, NAPO or the National Association of Senior Move Managers, NASMM. "Organizers bring a sense of orderliness with their ability to sort, group items, label, color code, and get rid of excess, to achieve a peaceful and balanced space." Michele Worthington.

Objects weigh you down. Give yourself the freedom to enjoy your living space free of stuff and at the same time give your family the benefit of having made these important decisions.

Another very important area of discussion is finances. Recently, a dear friend became ill and realized that she handled all the bill paying in the home, managed the bank accounts, and kept important papers in a safe deposit box, yet her husband had no knowledge of any of this. She immediately wrote a list of all the bank accounts, where they were located, where the safe deposit box was located, as well as a list of passwords.

In many families, husbands handle all finances and never share the information with their wives or children. If dementia should set in, or death occurs, the family is left to search out whatever information they can to take care of the remaining encumbrances. Recently I learned of a couple who had been married for sixty years and had separate bank accounts their entire married life. When the wife became ill, the husband had no idea which bank his wife used, what automatic payments were made from the accounts, and did not even have authorization to access the accounts.

Spare your family of such a nightmare. Make a list of all your bank accounts, what is automatically paid from which account, and the passwords or pin numbers to access these accounts. Also include where you keep the key to any safe deposit box. Keep this list with your important papers such as your Trust, and be sure to update the list whenever you change banks or circumstances change regarding your finances. Be sure to include your birth certificates and passports with your important papers as well.

Are you thinking of where you shall begin? Remember, one corner, one hour, one day will get you started. Your Journal is waiting!

What About Personal Treasures?

From the time we are young we go through many stages. As your family grows, we realize that some possessions are more important than others. Gifts that we may have received when we were younger or first married may no longer be important or useful to many families. What often comes to mind is silver serving trays and serving pieces. Sterling silver flatware sets will always hold their value and often are treasured and passed down from generation to generation. Silver serving pieces were often abundantly given as engagement and wedding gifts as well. I recently heard a 75 year woman express that her daughters and granddaughters would not want that kind of "stuff" anymore since it takes so much time to clean and polish. When asked if she had ever asked them, she said no.

Upon hearing this and realizing I had not ever asked my daughter or daughters-in-law how they felt, I promptly did so. To my utter surprise, my daughter told me that she absolutely would love to have some of the beautiful serving pieces. My daughters-in-law said the same thing and my 20 something granddaughters expressed their desire to also have some of the pieces. What a surprise, just when I was ready to sell a number of pieces to make room for more day-to-day trays. After hearing from them, I decided to label who gets what for each one of my girls and grandsons as well, in the event they too would like a piece of "grandma".

Getting back to our discussion about silver pieces, here is a bit of education about silver from the *Orlando Estate Buyer* in Winter Park, Florida.

A piece of silver that is truly sterling silver has greater monetary worth, and has markings somewhere on the bottom that must say "sterling" or the numbers "925" on US silver. If you see "International Silver", "Community Plate" or "E.P." or "E.P.N.S.", it is a plated item. Same thing goes for "extra plate", "triple plate", or "quadruple-plate". All are plated items. One of the main reasons for their lower value is that the layers of silver on plated items over time will wear off after use and cleaning, exposing the metal underneath and eventually becoming unusable. Genuine silver keeps it luster forever if cleaned and covered properly.

In my experience, keeping all pieces of silver and silver plate covered or contained in plastic generally keeps them tarnish free for a longer period of time. Silver plate was used from the early 1900's due to the cost and availability of sterling. Unfortunately, silver plate today does not have much monetary value. The importance of it is in the value it may hold to a loved one who remembers those special dinners or may wish to have them to make their own dinners beautiful and special.

Furniture that is 100 years old or older is considered antique. Fifty to 99 years is considered Vintage and less than 50 is considered a collectible. For more information, check Pamela *Wiggins' Buying and Selling Antiques and Collectibles on eBay*. If you have furniture that falls into those categories, remember to mark them as well. If you wish to find out the value of these pieces contact a local Antique House and ask for an appraiser to come to your home. These pieces are your treasures and you should decide who gets which piece.

If you are not sure of the value of something precious and believe that it is old and perhaps worth a great deal, contact an Auction House. Auction houses specialize in just about everything these days. If you are interested in selling, the auction representative, who acts as a non-biased third party, has many avenues in which to sell an item due to long term relationships with private clients and on-line real time bidding—which is done quite often. The Auction representative offers an appraisal value and will put your things up for sale. This mechanism can be used when families wish to sell items without the hassle but reap the benefit. Public auctions can be held. Auctioneers require fees or a percentage of the sale and handle everything associated with the auction.

If you want to sell items but do not want strangers coming to your home, consignment stores take items in very good condition. There are specialty consignment stores that will come to your home and appraise the items and often make an offer to purchase the entire collection. It is often worth taking a few dollars less if the consignment store will haul all the items to their store for you, saving you the hassle of having to move them yourself.

There are specialty charities such as RECARES which takes used medical equipment. The Salvation Army will pick up one piece of furniture or large estates. When donating to a charity, it is always good to know that what you donate will benefit others. When donating to religious organizations, be sure to contact the specific organization to learn about their regulations enabling them to accept such a gift. Carefully consider other personal treasures such as family heirlooms—which are especially difficult to part with—and choose a loved one who will appreciate and treasure such a gift.

Audrey writes: "While I was pregnant with my first son, I knitted a small, white scalloped edged baby afghan. I wrapped my baby boy in that afghan to bring him home and used it during his infancy. I did the same with my second son. I passed on the

Audrey with baby David wrapped in the afghan she hand knitted.

afghan to my youngest sister, who used the afghan to bring both her children home. I saved that afghan and it was used to bring each of my eldest son's two children home from the hospital as well. I have since vacuumed sealed that afghan with a note explaining its family history and significance and hope that it be used should there be more grandchildren or great grandchildren in years to come. It brought me great joy to have had my handiwork used as it has been in my family. It is a small piece of my legacy that I hope to leave in my family's hearts and minds."

Have you something you want to leave to the future generations? Start writing!

Your Wishes, Your Choice!

Managing Conflicts

What most of us are afraid of is making a mistake and choosing one person over another when deciding, "who gets what". Remember this process is about you making decisions.

If you recall earlier, one person called together her daughters and let them choose, stating the parameters. She hoped that this would avoid arguments, but if the daughters could not agree she would make the final decision. Then they would only find out the decision after she was gone. You can decide to bring your family together or made the decisions on your own. We know the personalities of our family members. Some relatives are more agreeable than others, and bringing them together to make decisions can go either way. It is for you to decide.

Another way to avoid conflict is to make all the decisions by yourself. If you wish to include your family in the decision-making process, ask for their input and let them know that you will take all of it into consideration, but the final decision will ultimately be yours.

Betty writes: "I have come to the realization that few family members will value my possessions and their meanings to me in the way that I myself do. That is just the nature of the things we collect in our lifetimes. So, I feel that I need to groom and choose the recipients of some of my more meaningful possessions so that they value and appreciate what will someday become theirs".

Disagreements and conflicts in families are not unusual. It is the way in which we handle these conflicts that is important, and that often depends upon the way in which we listen. Therapists suggest that we listen before making a decision. When we listen we give family members and others with whom we communicate all the respect deserved, telling them we care about their ideas and thoughts. When family members realize they are being heard, potential conflicts disappear.

Helene wrote: "My Dad and his brother had the best idea I have ever heard, they drew numbers, one and two, and then they alternated in picking."

Often we make decisions based on our relationships. You may feel closer to a family member you see frequently than one you see infrequently because of distance. Different people have different values and expectations, and when living apart, we do not always know or understand those values or their expectations. If your close family members live in multiple states and visits are limited, you may consider making the decisions yourself to avoid further conflict.

For those of us who do not have family members available—no children, nieces, or cousins—think seriously about how you would like to dispose of your special treasurers.

In my recent survey, those people who did not have any close family suggested leaving a few things to close friends. They let their estate plan designate the recipients and what they would get. They suggested the rest go to auction, with any monetary gain donated to a religious organization or the charity of their choice.

If you decide to leave your estate to a charity, be sure to check first with your legal and financial advisor. There are a number of ways to leave your estate to charity and avoid paying higher tax consequences and probate charges. Also contact the charity to learn about their needs and how they would like the bequest stated.

Your Journal, is awaiting your words, your thoughts, your gifts. Your wishes, your choice…

PART II
LEGAL

CHAPTER FIVE

LEGAL TIPS ON TRUSTS, WILLS, POWERS OF ATTORNEY, AND MORE

B
ecause the laws of each state are different, this topic can only be presented in broad generalities. You should consult with legal counsel in your state to confirm accurate information. When considering estate planning—wills, trusts, etc.—people generally consider only the inevitable death scenario; disregarding the possibility of mental or physical incapacity as a prelude to the inevitable. Given the aging of our population, incapacity has become a looming reality for many seniors, and planning for that contingency needs to be addressed.

Powers of Attorney

There are two types of powers of attorney—health care and financial matters. The power of attorney for health care grants the agent (the individual chosen for this position) the authority to make all decisions for a (normally) mentally incapacitated principal. This is defined as the person asking for the power of attorney, and pertaining to the principal's personal needs and care, including health care decisions. Normally this type of power of attorney grants authority for the agent to make decisions upon the principal losing mental capacity to such a degree that the person is unable to make medical decisions for themselves. This is called a "springing" power of attorney, because the authority springs into effectiveness upon the principal losing mental capacity. However, it can also be created as a "immediate" power of attorney granting the agent the immediate authority to make these kinds of decisions even though the principal is legally capable of doing so themselves.

For instance, where an elder parent is uncomfortable making those decisions all by themselves because of mental or emotional impairment.

The health care power of attorney can be very broad and general, or it can be very specific. In either event, the agent's authority is limited to that granted by the document.

The power of attorney for financial matters works very much like the health care power of attorney, but rather than addressing the issues of personal care and needs, the financial power of attorney addresses financial, property and legal matters. Like its counterpart, the power of attorney for financial matters can be very broad and general, or very specific. Powers of attorney are often drafted to grant only specific authority—such as for the purpose of selling a parcel of real property, or for a particular transaction, or type of transaction. These are appropriate under specific circumstances, but not sufficient as an estate-planning tool because they are too limited. When preparing a financial power of attorney for estate planning circumstances it is impossible to anticipate all of the millions of potential situations which might arise and draft a document accordingly. Therefore, the document needs to be drafted very broadly by necessity.

Powers of attorney can be immediately effective upon execution or springing. The springing powers of attorney, whether for health care or financial affairs, become effective upon the happening of some contingency, such as the principal losing mental capacity to handle their own affairs. Springing powers of attorney contingent upon lack of mental capacity remain effective for so long as the principal lacks mental capacity. For instance, during the period of a surgery while the principal is anesthetized. But upon the principal recovering from the anesthetic, regaining capacity, and able to make their own decisions, the authority of the agent lapses

So why do we need powers of attorney as part of an estate plan? Because if someone loses mental capacity who then can make medical or financial decisions on their behalf? People often assume that their spouse will be able to make those decisions on their behalf during any period of mental incapacity. Whether or not this is true depends upon the laws of the particular state where you reside. Most states grant limited authority for one spouse to make medical decisions for their spouse in emergency situations where decisions need to be made quickly. However, once the emergency circumstances have passed, this authority lapses. In that event, a court proceeding will likely be required whereby a court grants someone the authority to make the medical and financial decisions for someone who is incapacitated. In some states this is called a conservatorship, and in other states, a guardianship. In either event this is an ongoing legal process often requiring periodic accountings. It may require one to obtain additional authority to make specific kinds of decisions not granted within the general authority.

If someone loses mental capacity but has executed medical and financial powers of attorney, there is no need to resort to the conservatorship/guardianship process. Thus eliminating all of the cost and complications associated with them.

Powers of a Trustee

If a person has executed a trust, why would they need to also sign a power of attorney for financial affairs? The reason is that the trustee of a trust only has authority over the assets held in the name of the trust, and there may be a multitude of legal and financial matters that have nothing to do with trust assets. For instance, the trustee of a trust has no authority to file income tax returns for a beneficiary of the trust. Some assets can or should not ever be titled in the name of the trust. Also, if the beneficiary of a trust is injured in an accident caused by someone else, the legal action brought to recover damages for the injuries can't be brought by the trustee, but must be brought in the individual capacity of the injured person.

As an example, if someone were to change the title of their IRA, taking title in the name of the trustees of their trust, the IRS considers that IRA to be immediately terminated and the entire contents of the IRA be treated as if it had been withdrawn; subjecting all of it to immediate income taxation. Also, certain assets are prohibited from being held or transferred to a trust. Case in point, employee

Attorney and client meeting to discuss estate planning.

stock options normally include provisions prohibiting their transfer prior to being exercised. Thus if the employee loses mental capacity, the person holding their power of attorney for financial affairs can deal with those options appropriately.

Long Term Care Insurance

Two hundred years ago, people were not concerned with long term care due to physical or mental incapacity. With the advances of the medical sciences, people are living longer and the possibility of needing such care has increased dramatically. Our society hasn't really done a good job of addressing this change. Too few people properly plan for periods when they will need heightened care from another as they become less independently capable due to physical or mental conditions.

Long-term care insurance may be the solution for many people. The drawback it that this type of insurance is usually very expensive if not purchased early, so it becomes for many people beyond their means to afford. Others simply decide not to worry about it and let happen what happens. If you are able to purchase long-term care, it will provide a measure of comfort to know that you will have help in paying for care in the future.

Medicaid

The federal government has passed the Medicaid law, which enables each state to create their own public assistance program designed to help people pay for medical and skilled nursing home costs for which they are unable to pay. However, this is not an entitlement program like social security for which you can qualify notwithstanding your income and assets. To qualify for Medicaid, your income and assets can't exceed certain levels, and until your assets have been depleted below those levels, you will not qualify for this public assistance. The rules regarding what assets you can have and still qualify for these programs vary widely from state to state; as do the rules pertaining to what happens if you have transferred (gifted) away assets in order to qualify for this type of assistance. This is a boutique area of the law, requiring special training and skills to be able to guide you through this process. However, if you have lost mental capacity, who can undertake planning actions expediting your qualification? Typical powers of attorney do not include sufficient authority to undertake gifting or other strategies granting this kind of authority to undertake these types of planning decisions. It is very important that any power of attorney for financial affairs be carefully drafted, including specific authority covering the different situations which might occur in these scenarios.

Inheriting Assets

Upon a person's death, someone will inherit his or her assets. The laws of the individual states dictate how this can occur, and those can vary greatly. But there are some generalities that might apply.

Certain assets will not require any special legal proceedings, but will pass to heirs because of contract terms or designations. For instance, life insurance becomes payable to the beneficiaries upon the death of the insured. No special legal process needs to be undertaken. The beneficiaries simply file a claim form and prove the death by submission of a death certificate. Then the proceeds are paid in accordance with the provisions of the contract.

Retirement accounts, such as IRA, 401k and 401(b) are payable to the beneficiary designations made by the decedent, and are distributed upon filing a claim without further legal process.

Many assets will pass to the survivors based upon the nature of how title is held. For instance, an asset held as joint tenants among several people will automatically pass by "right of title" to the survivors when one of them passes away. Again, this is likely to be achieved by merely proving the death and further action is not required. Further examples are property held as tenants by the entirety, and community property with right of survivorship. Depending upon state laws, title to real property as well as financial accounts can be held in this fashion.

Many states have now implemented laws which allow financial accounts with banks and brokerage houses to have pre-designated beneficiaries in the event of the death of the owner. They are often referred to as "pay on death" or "transfer on death" provisions. Once again, no legal process is normally required beyond proving the death by submission of a death certificate.

What is Probate?

If an individual holds real, personal or intangible property in their name alone, (such that upon their death title will not pass by right of survivorship); and if there is no other provision (such as a pay on death designation) which will automatically pass title to designated heirs, most states will require that some legal process will have to be undertaken to garner the decedent's assets, apply those assets to pay off their existing debts, determine who has the legal right to inherit the remainder, and distribute the assets to those persons. This legal process is often called a probate.

Most states have alternative procedures for the administration of small estates. What is a small estate varies widely from state to state, and is controlled by the law where the real property is located—or in the case of property other than real property—by the law of the residence of the decedent.

Unless some alternative procedure is available, a full probate will have to be implemented. This can be very costly and often takes months if not years to complete. During the interim, assets are not normally distributed but are held in trust to be distributed at the very end of the process.

A method of avoiding probate is to transfer assets to a living trust. Upon the death of the trustor(s), the successor trustee passes on the assets without the necessity of probate.

In addition to avoiding probate, the living trust is used as a tool to achieve other goals, such as:

1. For married couples, doubling the amount of assets which can be passed by a married couple to the next generation by implementing an A/B or A/B/C format;

2. Assuring that the assets of the first spouse to die of a married couple pass to the chosen heirs of that spouse once the surviving spouse has passed away;

3. Controlling the disposition of assets among specific heirs, and the timing and method by which they will inherit;

4. Passing assets on to multiple generations, achieving a 'generation skip' which can have substantial estate tax advantages for following generations; and

5. Sheltering assets of special needs persons such that their inheritance will not interfere with any public assistance they might need, and yet remain available for their supplemental needs above and beyond what the public assistance programs will provide.

These goals and many more can be addressed in a good, thorough living trust, but are the subject of multiple volumes and beyond the scope of this one chapter.

It is never too early or too late to obtain a Living Trust. If you already have one, be sure to have it updated after a minimum of five years.

PART III
LIFE CHOICES

CHAPTER SIX

MAKING LIFE CHOICES

There are many things in life that are out of our control. A serious illness leaving one unable to speak or think clearly is certainly a major factor in one's life. Today, there are a number of ways to inform your doctor, healthcare providers, and family as to what your wishes are regarding your care.

Case study: "Mrs. Doe is conserved because of her severe dementia and has been a nursing home patient on Medi-Cal for more than five years. She has no family and left no written instructions about her health care wishes. In the past two years, she has become unable to walk or to follow any simple commands. She has not spoken in months. During the past year, she has required spoon-feeding, and she has been taking progressively longer to eat each meal. Because of episodes of coughing and possibly choking, her diet has been changed to puree with thick liquids. She still seems to prefer some foods and the staff can tell you which foods she will usually spit out. She has been hospitalized twice for pneumonia in the past year but has recovered without needing ICU treatment.

One Saturday evening, Mrs. Doe is congested. She begins running a fever, and her breathing seems labored. The nursing home staff calls 911 and sends the patient to the hospital. The emergency room physician consults with the internist and the pulmonologist and the patient goes to the intensive care unit. She is intubated and put on a ventilator. After two days of antibiotics and vigorous suctioning, she seems to be breathing better, but she has required restraint to keep her from pulling out the breathing tube and sedatives so she does not try to hit the ICU staff.

The physician comes to see Mrs. Doe in the ICU on Monday afternoon. On his way to see her, he gets a message that the nursing home has just called to see if Mrs. Doe will have a feeding tube placed while she is in the hospital. They point out that she has been losing weight and takes so long to eat a meal that it is impacting the staff's ability to get other jobs done. When he arrives in the ICU, the patient is still on the ventilator and each wrist has a binder that secures her to the bed frame. Although she is somewhat sedated, she seems uncomfortable and there is still and aura of panic that penetrates her drug haze.

The ICU physician is glad to see the physician because he has a lot of questions about what happens next with the patient." *Elizabeth Menkin, MD. Founder of Coda Alliance, a Silicon Valley community coalition for end-of-life care.*

The questions arise as to what should be done. Should Mrs. Doe be resuscitated if she suffers cardiac arrest? Should she continue to be kept restrained? Can the nursing home do IV antibiotics and even accept her back? These are just a few of the questions one would be asked to answer since Mrs. Doe does not have any previous directive and the decisions will not be hers, but that of her physician. The physician may or may not have the same religious beliefs as Mrs. Doe and therefore make decisions based on his beliefs not knowing hers.

I recently read that 60% of people say that making sure their family is not burdened by tough decisions is extremely important and yet only a small number of people have actually taken the steps necessary to see that such situations don't occur.

To help make these decisions doctors now have available a form known as a POLST or Physicians Order For Life Sustaining Treatment. The POLST is a physician order that helps gives seriously ill patients more control over their end-of-life care. The POLST specifies the types of medical treatment that a patient wishes to receive towards the end of life and can prevent unwanted or medically ineffective treatment, reduce patient and family suffering, and help ensure that patients' wishes are honored. The POLST is intended to be filled out with the help of your physician, and must be signed by your physician. It is important for you to think about it, and bring it to your physician's attention. This document is valid in a number of states, and can be requested at your health care providers. If you travel to another state, take an Advance Directive or Healthcare Power of Attorney and your POLST form with you. The POLST form complements an Advance Directive and is not intended to replace that document. An Advance Directive is still necessary to appoint a legal health care decision maker.

To learn about the POLST program go to polst.org. The POLST form is availabe on the web at *www.capolst.org*. In any state, I am sure your doctor would appreciate having this information in your chart, so do not hesitate to fill it out and give a copy to whomever you have chosen to be your healthcare provider. Have a discussion about your choices with your healthcare advocate. By completing this simple form, your doctor, family, and other health care providers are aware of how you want to be treated in the event of a serious or life threating illness. Family members often make decisions based on their personal relationship with the patient, or their own religious convictions not necessarily in conjunction with the patient's beliefs.

Go Wish Cards

The GO WISH card game is an advance care planning tool developed by Coda Alliance, the Silicon Valley (Santa Clara County, California) to help people have conversations about end-of-life care. The cards focus the conversations, provide important vocabulary to give voice to the participant's needs and concerns, and offer a way of sharing those ideas. The cards provide a wide selection of examples of situations with which the participant can agree, disagree, amend, or interpret. Go Wish cards give the reader an easy, even entertaining way to think and talk about how you want to be treated if you become seriously ill. The game can be used to help your friends and family understand your wishes and make it easier to follow them when the time comes. Coda's intention in developing the tool was to promote conversations well in advance of serious illness. It helps the participant and their families to have a better understanding of what their loved one wants. Go Wish Game by Coda Alliance can be purchased by going to the web site *www. codaalliance.org.* The cards have statements for discussion as to how one might feel about a particular statement such as "Not being a burden to my family" or " To feel that my life is complete" and "To have a doctor who knows me as a whole person." One can do this alone or with others and it certainly brings up some interesting thoughts that one may have never previously voiced.

Life Care Decisions

Many people believe that if they have a Trust, Healthcare Power of Attorney, or Will—all very important documents—they do not have to have any further health related documents. That is not the case. These documents do not always address some very important issues regarding sustaining life. You, as an individual, have the right to decide your own care in the event of a catastrophic illness, such as a stroke or life-threatening disease. Your family or Healthcare Power of Attorney may not address artificial medical treatments such as the necessity for feeding tubes when the quality of life is impaired and/or limited. These decisions should be made known when one is able to do so. Telling your children how you feel is very important. However, having it in writing ensures that your children will not forget or change the outcome if it is against your written instructions.

I hope the following explanation will be helpful in understanding and deciding what you would prefer in the event of a catastrophic event.

Life-Support treatment is defined as any medical treatment to keep one alive. Treatments may include devices to help breathe, food and water supplied by a feeding tube, CPR (cardiopulmonary resuscitation) to restart breathing, major surgery, blood transfusions, mechanical ventilation, which allows a pump to push air in and out of the lungs through a tube, and anything else meant to keep one alive. It does not take into consideration one's quality of life or religious preferences.

If you have a medical emergency and medical personnel are called to your home, for example, the emergency technician will look for any identifying instructions such as a medical bracelet, Vial of Life directive or a DNR (do not resuscitate) form. These forms will alert medical personnel as to exactly what you wish.

If you are no longer able to make your own decisions pertaining to your healthcare, recording your wishes as to treatment should be written allowing you to make your own choices. Once you record these choices, be sure to alert the person you choose to oversee your medical treatments what your wishes are and where to find the information you have written. Discussing this with your chosen person helps you to gain peace of mind that your wishes will be carried out. In the event that you choose a person, who for whatever the reason does not wish to take the responsibility— perhaps for religious reasons or anything else—choose another responsible person. It is important that you know the person you choose and trust will, in fact, carry out your wishes exactly as you have expressed.

Take a moment to go to the back of this book and write in the Journal what your specific wishes are regarding your care. Starting on page 79 *The Personal Journal* you will find some helpful questions to guide you through this process.

It is extremely important that you make your loved ones aware that you have recorded information pertaining to your treatment for any future illnesses, mental or physical incapacitation, or death, either in your Journal or in some other location. In the event you are unable to direct them in the future, it is *imperative* for them to know where this information is located.

PART IV
DECISON TOOLS

Chapter Seven

Life Decisions

Most people do not wish to talk about dying and everything having to do with end of life decisions. They will do everything and anything to avoid the conversation. When seniors are asked if they wish to avoid placing the burden of these decisions on their family members, however, the majority answer "absolutely". In reality, however, most of the senior population has not communicated their end of life choices to anyone.

To protect your family from the anguish of making these decisions for you and ensure that they know what your thoughts are regarding these important life decisons; please complete the "Life Decisions" questions at the beginning of your journal. These questions need your answers and are "for your eyes only" until you wish to share this information. Completing this form and having this conversation with your family unburdens them and is a most thoughtful and considerate personal gift.

The following pages offer questions as a guide to making these decisions. You may find as you were reading the chapters that more questions arise.. Feel free to add any information that you feel is important for your loved ones to know.

The suggestions offered in the previous chapters and the following pages, are to start you thinking about and recording the important information for your family and help avoid disappointment, conflict, frustration and division at a time when we hope to leave a loving legacy.

MY WISHES, MY CHOICE

THE PERSONAL JOURNAL

OF _____

Attention Computer and Tablet Users

Anyone wishing to download the PDF writable
version of The Personal Journal may do so by going
to www.whattodowithyourstuff.com

1. I have a Health Care Power of Attorney and it is located

_____

_____

2. I have completed a "Do Not Resuscitate" form and it is located

_____

_____

3. I have completed the Physicians' Order for Life Sustaining Treatment signed by my physician and it is located

_____

_____

4. I have chosen my healthcare agent and he/she is

_____

_____

_____ date _____

5. My healthcare agent can be located at

_____

_____

6. If this person is unable to do so, then I choose

_____

_____

_____ date _____

7. My alternate healthcare agent can be located at

_____

_____

9. I have a Trust and it is located _____

_____

_____

10. My Attorney's name is_____

_____

_____

11. My Attorney's address and telephone number is _____

_____

_____

12. My Durable Power of Attorney is located at

_____

_____

13. My Long Term Care Insurance Carrier is

_____

_____

14. My Long Term Care Insurance Information is located at

_____

_____

15. My Life Insurance is with what company _____

_____

_____

16. My Life Insurance Information is located in _____

_____

_____

17. My Life Insurance Agent's Address is _____

_____

_____

18. My Bank Accounts are located at _____

_____

_____

19. My Brokerage Accounts are located at _____

_____

_____

20. I have a Safe Deposit Box located at _____

_____

21. The directions to locate the key to the Safe Deposit Box can be found _____

_____

only after I am incapacitated and declared so by a doctor and/or death certificate.

22. I wish to have my Pasteur/Rabbi/Priest/Minister or _____

_____

_____ present at my passing.

23. My funeral wishes and burial information is known to _____

_____

_____

24. Record any further information you wish to share regarding personal choices. _____

_____

_____

_____

_____

25. Additional Notes may include "Things to be remembered about me" or "A Letter to my Loved Ones" or whatever you feel you would like to say to those you leave behind. _____

_____

_____

_____

_____

_____

_____

18. Many people wish to write their own obituary or list pertinent facts others might be unaware to list. If you wish to write your obituary or make particular facts known about your life, be sure to include that information here.

_____

_____

_____

_____

_____

_____

_____

_____

_____

_____

_____

_____

_____

_____

_____

_____

My Wishes As To Who Gets What

Your Item _____

Who is the Recipient _____

Why and/or a Story _____

_____

_____

_____

Your Item _____

Who is the Recipient _____

Why and/or a Story _____

_____

_____

_____

Your Item _____

Who is the Recipient _____

Why and/or a Story _____

_____

_____

_____

My Wishes As To Who Gets What

Your Item _____

Who is the Recipient _____

Why and/or a Story _____

_____

_____

_____

Your Item _____

Who is the Recipient _____

Why and/or a Story _____

_____

_____

_____

Your Item _____

Who is the Recipient _____

Why and/or a Story _____

_____

_____

_____

My Wishes As To Who Gets What

Your Item _____

Who is the Recipient _____

Why and/or a Story _____

_____

_____

_____

Your Item _____

Who is the Recipient _____

Why and/or a Story _____

_____

_____

_____

Your Item _____

Who is the Recipient _____

Why and/or a Story _____

_____

_____

_____

My Wishes As To Who Gets What

Your Item _____

Who is the Recipient _____

Why and/or a Story _____

_____

_____

_____

Your Item _____

Who is the Recipient _____

Why and/or a Story _____

_____

_____

_____

Your Item _____

Who is the Recipient _____

Why and/or a Story _____

_____

_____

_____

My Wishes As To Who Gets What

Your Item _____

Who is the Recipient _____

Why and/or a Story _____

_____

_____

_____

Your Item _____

Who is the Recipient _____

Why and/or a Story _____

_____

_____

_____

Your Item _____

Who is the Recipient _____

Why and/or a Story _____

_____

_____

_____

My Wishes As To Who Gets What

Your Item _____

Who is the Recipient _____

Why and/or a Story _____

_____

_____

_____

Your Item _____

Who is the Recipient _____

Why and/or a Story _____

_____

_____

_____

Your Item _____

Who is the Recipient _____

Why and/or a Story _____

_____

_____

_____

My Wishes As To Who Gets What

Your Item _____

Who is the Recipient _____

Why and/or a Story _____

_____

_____

_____

Your Item _____

Who is the Recipient _____

Why and/or a Story _____

_____

_____

_____

Your Item _____

Who is the Recipient _____

Why and/or a Story _____

_____

_____

_____

My Wishes As To Who Gets What

Your Item _____

Who is the Recipient _____

Why and/or a Story _____

_____

_____

_____

Your Item _____

Who is the Recipient _____

Why and/or a Story _____

_____

_____

_____

Your Item _____

Who is the Recipient _____

Why and/or a Story _____

_____

_____

_____

My Wishes As To Who Gets What

Your Item _____

Who is the Recipient _____

Why and/or a Story _____

_____

_____

_____

Your Item _____

Who is the Recipient _____

Why and/or a Story _____

_____

_____

_____

Your Item _____

Who is the Recipient _____

Why and/or a Story _____

_____

_____

_____

My Wishes As To Who Gets What

Your Item _____

Who is the Recipient _____

Why and/or a Story _____

_____

_____

_____

Your Item _____

Who is the Recipient _____

Why and/or a Story _____

_____

_____

_____

Your Item _____

Who is the Recipient _____

Why and/or a Story _____

_____

_____

_____

My Wishes As To Who Gets What

Your Item _____

Who is the Recipient _____

Why and/or a Story _____

_____

_____

_____

Your Item _____

Who is the Recipient _____

Why and/or a Story _____

_____

_____

_____

Your Item _____

Who is the Recipient _____

Why and/or a Story _____

_____

_____

_____

My Wishes As To Who Gets What

Your Item _____

Who is the Recipient _____

Why and/or a Story _____

_____

_____

_____

Your Item _____

Who is the Recipient _____

Why and/or a Story _____

_____

_____

_____

Your Item _____

Who is the Recipient _____

Why and/or a Story _____

_____

_____

_____

Physician Orders for Life-Sustaining Treatment (POLST)

First follow these orders, then contact physician.
A copy of the signed POLST form is a legally valid physician order. Any section not completed implies full treatment for that section. **POLST complements** an Advance Directive **and is not intended to replace that document.**

EMSA #111 B
(Effective 10/1/2014)*

Patient Last Name:	Date Form Prepared:
Patient First Name:	Patient Date of Birth:
Patient Middle Name:	Medical Record #: *(optional)*

A	CARDIOPULMONARY RESUSCITATION (CPR): *If patient has no pulse and is not breathing.*
Check One	*If patient is NOT in cardiopulmonary arrest, follow orders in Sections B and C.*

☐ **Attempt Resuscitation/CPR** (Selecting CPR in Section A **requires** selecting Full Treatment in Section B)
☐ **Do Not Attempt Resuscitation/DNR** (Allow Natural Death)

B	MEDICAL INTERVENTIONS: *If patient is found with a pulse and/or is breathing.*

Check One

☐ **Full Treatment** – primary goal of prolonging life by all medically effective means.
In addition to treatment described in Selective Treatment and Comfort-Focused Treatment, use intubation, advanced airway interventions, mechanical ventilation, and cardioversion as indicated.
  ☐ *Trial Period of Full Treatment.*

☐ **Selective Treatment** – goal of treating medical conditions while avoiding burdensome measures.
In addition to treatment described in Comfort-Focused Treatment, use medical treatment, IV antibiotics, and IV fluids as indicated. Do not intubate. May use non-invasive positive airway pressure. Generally avoid intensive care.
  ☐ *Request transfer to hospital only if comfort needs cannot be met in current location.*

☐ **Comfort-Focused Treatment** – primary goal of maximizing comfort.
Relieve pain and suffering with medication by any route as needed; use oxygen, suctioning, and manual treatment of airway obstruction. Do not use treatments listed in Full and Selective Treatment unless consistent with comfort goal. *Request transfer to hospital only if comfort needs cannot be met in current location.*

Additional Orders: _____

C	ARTIFICIALLY ADMINISTERED NUTRITION: *Offer food by mouth if feasible and desired.*

Check One

☐ Long-term artificial nutrition, including feeding tubes.   Additional Orders: _____
☐ Trial period of artificial nutrition, including feeding tubes. _____
☐ No artificial means of nutrition, including feeding tubes. _____

D	INFORMATION AND SIGNATURES:

Discussed with: ☐ Patient (Patient Has Capacity)   ☐ Legally Recognized Decisionmaker

☐ Advance Directive dated _____, available and reviewed →   Healthcare Agent if named in Advance Directive:
☐ Advance Directive not available   Name: _____
☐ No Advance Directive   Phone: _____

Signature of Physician
My signature below indicates to the best of my knowledge that these orders are consistent with the patient's medical condition and preferences.

Print Physician Name:	Physician Phone Number:	Physician License Number:
Physician Signature: *(required)*		Date:

Signature of Patient or Legally Recognized Decisionmaker
I am aware that this form is voluntary. By signing this form, the legally recognized decisionmaker acknowledges that this request regarding resuscitative measures is consistent with the known desires of, and with the best interest of, the patient who is the subject of the form.

Print Name:	Relationship: *(write self if patient)*
Signature: *(required)*	Date:
Mailing Address (street/city/state/zip):	Phone Number:	Office Use Only:

*Form versions with effective dates of 1/1/2009 or 4/1/2011 are also valid

Patient Information

Name (last, first, middle):	Date of Birth:	Gender: M F

Healthcare Provider Assisting with Form Preparation ☐ N/A if POLST is completed by signing physician

Name:	Title:	Phone Number:

Additional Contact ☐ None

Name:	Relationship to Patient:	Phone Number:

Directions for Healthcare Provider

Completing POLST

- **Completing a POLST form is voluntary.** California law requires that a POLST form be followed by healthcare providers, and provides immunity to those who comply in good faith. In the hospital setting, a patient will be assessed by a physician who will issue appropriate orders that are consistent with the patient's preferences.
- **POLST does not replace the Advance Directive.** When available, review the Advance Directive and POLST form to ensure consistency, and update forms appropriately to resolve any conflicts.
- POLST must be completed by a healthcare provider based on patient preferences and medical indications.
- A legally recognized decisionmaker may include a court-appointed conservator or guardian, agent designated in an Advance Directive, orally designated surrogate, spouse, registered domestic partner, parent of a minor, closest available relative, or person whom the patient's physician believes best knows what is in the patient's best interest and will make decisions in accordance with the patient's expressed wishes and values to the extent known.
- A legally recognized decisionmaker may execute the POLST form only if the patient lacks capacity or has designated that the decisionmaker's authority is effective immediately.
- POLST must be signed by a physician and the patient or decisionmaker to be valid. Verbal orders are acceptable with follow-up signature by physician in accordance with facility/community policy.
- If a translated form is used with patient or decisionmaker, attach it to the signed English POLST form.
- Use of original form is strongly encouraged. Photocopies and FAXes of signed POLST forms are legal and valid. A copy should be retained in patient's medical record, on Ultra Pink paper when possible.

Using POLST

- Any incomplete section of POLST implies full treatment for that section.

Section A:
- If found pulseless and not breathing, no defibrillator (including automated external defibrillators) or chest compressions should be used on a patient who has chosen "Do Not Attempt Resuscitation."

Section B:
- When comfort cannot be achieved in the current setting, the patient, including someone with "Comfort-Focused Treatment," should be transferred to a setting able to provide comfort (e.g., treatment of a hip fracture).
- Non-invasive positive airway pressure includes continuous positive airway pressure (CPAP), bi-level positive airway pressure (BiPAP), and bag valve mask (BVM) assisted respirations.
- IV antibiotics and hydration generally are not "Comfort-Focused Treatment."
- Treatment of dehydration prolongs life. If a patient desires IV fluids, indicate "Selective Treatment" or "Full Treatment."
- Depending on local EMS protocol, "Additional Orders" written in Section B may not be implemented by EMS personnel.

Reviewing POLST

It is recommended that POLST be reviewed periodically. Review is recommended when:
- The patient is transferred from one care setting or care level to another, or
- There is a substantial change in the patient's health status, or
- The patient's treatment preferences change.

Modifying and Voiding POLST

- A patient with capacity can, at any time, request alternative treatment or revoke a POLST by any means that indicates intent to revoke. It is recommended that revocation be documented by drawing a line through Sections A through D, writing "VOID" in large letters, and signing and dating this line.
- A legally recognized decisionmaker may request to modify the orders, in collaboration with the physician, based on the known desires of the patient or, if unknown, the patient's best interests.

This form is approved by the California Emergency Medical Services Authority in cooperation with the statewide POLST Task Force. For more information or a copy of the form, visit **www.caPOLST.org.**

SEND FORM WITH PATIENT WHENEVER TRANSFERRED OR DISCHARGED

Resources

Anderson, Linda. "Why Is It So Hard To Let Go Of All That Stuff?"— *Attention Deficit Disorder Association.* August 16, 2014, with permission *http://www.add.org/page/stuff*

Dyas, Brie. "Pack Rat Or Hoarder? Here Are The 6 Signs that Tell The Difference". *Huffington Post.* April 12, 2014 *http://www.huffingtonpost.com/2013/09/06/hoarder-signs_n_3867423.html*

Fricke, Diane. "Uncovering the History Behind Collecting". *HorizonLines.org*

Goldberg, Stan. *The 10 Rules of Change,* Psychology Today. July 24, 2014 *http://www.psychologytoday.com/articles/200210/the-1-rules-change*

Live Smart After 50. LIFE PLANNING NETWORK, Boston, Massachusetts *www.LiveSmartAfter50.com*

Menkin, Elizabeth S. "Go Wish: A Tool For End-of-Life Care Conversations". *Journal of Pallative Medicine.* April, 2007. http://www.codaalliance.org/

Nichols, Diane. "Precious Pearls" *For Women First.* February 17, 2014, with permission

Sapadin, Linda. "Can People Really Change?", World of Psychology. July 24, 2014 *http://www.psychcentral.com/blog/archives/2014/03/02/can-people-really-change/*

Szalavitz, Maria. "Why Older People Tend to be Poor Decisionmakers." Time.com. January 20, 2014 *http://healthland.time.com/2013/09/30/why-older-people-tend-to-be-poor-decions-makers/*

Thomas, Bill. *Second Wind.* Simon & Schuster. 2014

About the Author

Lois started her journey working with seniors when her beloved sister, Judy, was diagnosed with early onset Alzheimer's disease in her mid fifties. Lois has become an innovative leader on the subject of senior issues and caring for loved ones with Alzheimer's disease. She is a well known public speaker regarding geriatric care as well as how it relates to long-term care and the law and is a resource for seniors in areas such as dementia, Medicare, Medi-Cal/Medicaid, and Social Security. Lois has published in the Society of Senior Advisors Journal on Sundown Syndrome, authored a column called "Ask Lois" for the Monterey Alzheimer's Association Newsletter and wrote for "Senior Corner" the Campbell on-line "Patch" and Active Over 50 magazine. She has written numerous articles for "Elder Law Today," a newsletter for clients of the firm. For ten years, Lois was a volunteer facilitator for caregivers groups for Alzheimer's and Dementia."

Lois holds a Masters in Education from Providence College, specializing in counseling, a BS in Education from Boston University, and is a Certified Senior Advisor. She maintained a private practice for many years in counseling, taught at West Valley College in Saratoga, CA and Chabot College, Hayward, CA in Healthcare and presently is the Director of Geriatric Care Management for an estate planning law firm. Her life experiences have largely contributed to her desire and success in working with seniors and their families.

Presently, Lois lives in Saratoga, California with her husband. Together they raised five children and are blessed with seven grandchildren.

Index

Made in the USA
Coppell, TX
10 January 2023

10841983R00075